22— — EULENBURG AUDIO+SCORE

Felix Mendelssohn Bartholdy

2 Overtures

A Midsummer Night's Dream / Ein Sommernachtstraum Op. 21

The Hebrides / Die Hebriden Op. 26

Edited by / Herausgegeben von
Richard Clarke

EULENBURG

EAS 122
ISBN 978-3-7957-6522-4
ISMN M-2002-2345-3

Edition based on Eulenburg Study Score ETP 613 and 637

Ernst Eulenburg Ltd
48 Great Marlborough Street
London W1F 7BB

Contents / Inhalt

Preface

Felix Weingartner, writing in 1909, notes perceptively that 'had Mendelssohn given to his single-movement orchestral pieces the felicitous title "Symphonic Poems", which Liszt later invented, he would perhaps be celebrated today as the creator of program music and would take his place at the dawn of a new artistic era and not at the end of an old one. He would now be known as the "first modern" instead of the "last classic" composer'.

The 18th-century operatic overture was the parent to two offspring. The symphony, whose origins are not outwardly so obvious, began with the three-movement Italian opera overture of the Baroque and grew, as a result of Haydn's and Beethoven's adoption, into the four-movement grand gesture of serious abstract music. Again with Beethoven, the cord linking the overture with theatre and opera was once again severed as one can see among his output of ten or so examples. Naturally there are ballet and theatre overtures such as *Prometheus* or *Egmont*, but *Coriolan* Op. 62 – written for a play – had interestingly been unveiled in a concert at the palace of Prince Lobkowitz in March 1807, ahead of any stage performance, making it the first *de facto* concert overture.

But Beethoven's concert overtures – which also include Op. 115, a work 'zu jeder Gelegenheit oder zum Gebrauch im Konzert' (for any occasion of for concert use) – were not the programmatic works that were to prepare the way for the symphonic poem later in the 19th century. Weber and Schubert had written overtures that exist, in the case of the former, as remodelled independent overtures from unsuccessful operas and, with the latter, as a sequence of examples of early orchestral muscle-flexing.

The works that Mendelssohn published together in one volume as *Three Concert Overtures*, in 1835, in contrast seem to mark the induction of a new genre. Certainly the *Hebrides* overture was conceived very much as a 'tone picture' in response to his tour of the Western Isles in Scotland, not altogether unrelated to his *Meeresstille und glückliche Fahrt* (Calm Sea and Prosperous Voyage) in the same set. But the *Midsummer Night's Dream* does voice an off-stage echo – although the composer had not intended the work to be performed as a prelude to performances of Shakespeare's play. Nonetheless in 1826 and at the age of seventeen Mendelssohn had, perhaps more so than Beethoven, begun to see the way to developing a new form and genre of musical composition.

Berlioz had, after Mendelssohn's *Midsummer Night's Dream* and before its publication with *Hebrides* and *Meeresstille*, written a series of overtures – while less programmatic – which helped to establish this new genre through examples such as *Waverley* and the *Intrata di Rob-Roy* and indeed the Shakespearean *Le roi Lear* 'grande ouverture'. There are examples by Schumann, the English composer Sterndale Bennett and of course Wagner – including a *Faust* overture in 1840, later revised. Mendelssohn led the way, just escaping the fringe of Beethoven's shadow, in bringing the programmatic concert overture into being and, indeed, allowing for Liszt to cultivate the symphonic poem in the 1840s and 1850s.

Overture to A Midsummer Night's Dream *Op. 21*

Composed: 1826 in Berlin
First performance: Private performance at the Mendelssohn House, Berlin, during November 1826; first public performance in Stettin (Szczecin) on 20 February 1827 directed by Carl Loewe
Original publisher: Breitkopf & Härtel, Leipzig, parts 1832, score 1835
Instrumentation: 2 Flutes, 2 Oboes, 2 Clarinets, 2 Bassoons – 2 Horns, 2 Trumpets, Ophicleide – Timpani – Strings
Duration: ca. 12 minutes

'Music, ho! Music, such as charmeth sleep' says Titania in Act IV of Shakespeare's *A Midsummer Night's Dream*; and it is the seemingly dreamlike distant rustling of a sprite's wings, after four swelling wind chords, that conjures the sleepy vision at the beginning of Mendelssohn's overture. Opera overtures had often begun with a slow introduction, here reduced to the briefest of gestures, as can be found in Rossini's examples and indeed for instance in Beethoven's *Coriolan*.

Although this music mirrors closely the events of Shakespeare's play, the composer still hems in his ideas through the agency of a conventional musical structure – sonata form. Following the opening chords, the exposition (bb.8–250) of the overture gives us four themes. The first subject group, in the tonic key of E major, comprises the playful shimmering dance of the spirits and fairies of the Athenian woods and the grand *fortissimo* evocation of the palace of Theseus from Act I of the play (b.62) – followed with a distinctive descending scale in minims that appears in various guises throughout the work. The divided *pp* strings here is wonderfully subtle orchestration, a testament to the composer's early skill and imagination; the abrupt change to a full-orchestra *ff* is similarly dextrous. The second subject group, in the dominant key, has the chorale-like lovers' theme – portraying Hermia and Lysander, Helena and Demetrius – opening out into the phrase with its chromatically falling third; the violins' and flutes' *fortissimo* swagger in thirds, over the pounding octave Bs, at b.197, seems to depict the group of rustics who later on enact the 'play within a play' of *Pyramus and Thisbe* in Act V. We have here also the braying of Nick Bottom, in his ass's-head mask at Act III scene I, in swooping 10ths at b.214. There is of course no exposition repeat – in a 'narrative' work such as this that follows a borrowed story, it would make little sense – and overture sonata form, from Beethoven's time, indeed did not demonstrate such a feature.

The subdued *p/pp* development section of the work places us squarely within the Athenian woods that form the backdrop to the central acts of Shakespeare's play. The return of the first theme informs us that we are without doubt in Oberon's fairy kingdom and the descending scale that answers the second theme in the exposition lures us further into the forest with stealthy pizzicato crotchets in octave unison violins and cellos. The broken hearted fragmentary allusion to the close of the lovers' theme – like the shattered fragments of melody in the cavatina of Beethoven's String Quartet in B flat op. 130 – shares with us the ill-fated affections at the close of the development, as the overture's opening chords appear for a second time ahead of the recapitulation.

The recapitulation omits its reference to the splendour of Theseus's palace after the *pianissimo* fairies' dance and instead this first theme's recurrence is elided with the end of the transition from the exposition, leading us straight into the lovers' theme again – this time, naturally, in the tonic. As in Act V, the last act of Shakespeare's play, Quince, Bottom, Snout et al step forward to present their play with Mendelssohn's *fortissimo* octave E drone and musette-style rustic revelry – complete with Bottom, in his ass's mask, braying in 9ths and 10ths. As before, this is deft handling of the string section, since he infers the use of portamenti for joyous quasi-comical effect. Theseus does finally appear, however, at b.586 with stretto fanfares thrown between winds and strings (bb.597–606). The coda of the overture slips quietly into the twilit, sylvan world of the fairies with the strings' rapid quavers once more and the held chords broadened out still further. The grand second theme appears a final time, very quietly transformed into a reference to Carl Maria von Weber's opera *Oberon*. A Mermaid's Song from Act II of Weber's work is echoed at b.663 – closely reflecting Weber's 6/8 song in the triplets at b.667–9. It is as if Mendelssohn here '… heard a mermaid on a dolphin's back / Uttering such dulcet … breath / That the rude sea grew civil at her song' (Oberon, *A Midsummer Night's Dream*, Act II, scene i). And so the opening chords return one third and final time to close the work, in quiet mystery – to 'disappear with the dawn' as Mendelssohn later described it to the publishers Breitkopf & Härtel.

The first public orchestral performance of the overture took place on 20 February 1827 in modern-day Szczecin (then Stettin), although it had been heard at the Mendelssohns' own home in 1826, not long after its composition in that year. Begun at some point in the first half of July the score was completed, so the autograph tells us, on 6 August. The work had existed first in a piano duet version, and it was in this form that the composer Ignaz Moscheles reports hearing it in November 1826. The composer clearly continued to value the overture, since he both conducted it regularly at concerts, including London, and returned to it sixteen years later. In 1842 he added additional movements of incidental music for Shakespeare's play – including a Nocturne, a Scherzo and a Wedding March – in response to a commission from King Friedrich Wilhelm IV of Prussia. When the *Overture to A Midsummer Night's Dream* was published along with *Hebrides* and *Meeresstille* seven years earlier, it had been to Friedrich Wilhelm, at the time Crown Prince, that the composer had then dedicated the work.

David Lewiston Sharpe

Overture The Hebrides *Op. 26*

Composed: 1830–33
First performance: 14 May 1832, Philharmonic Society, London, directed by the composer
Original publisher: Breitkopf & Härtel, Leipzig, parts 1834, score 1835
Instrumentation: 2 Flutes, 2 Oboes, 2 Clarinets, 2 Bassoons – 2 Horns, 2 Trumpets – Timpani – Strings
Duration: ca. 11 minutes

At Fort William, early on Friday 7 August 1829, Mendelssohn and his friend Carl Klingemann caught one of the new paddle-steamers that were running between Inverness and Glasgow through the recently-opened Caledonian Canal, and it took them forty miles down Loch Linnhe to Oban, through some of the loveliest scenery in Europe. Mendelssohn was twenty at the time. From Oban Harbour he walked a mile up the coast and began a pencil sketch of a mediaeval ruin called Dunollie Castle; he was able to include Loch Linnhe and the distant mountains of Mull in the background. He did not have time to finish the sketch because they had another steamer to catch. That evening they embarked for Iona on the *Ben Lomond* (70 tons) which took them from Oban as far as Tobermory, Mull's only harbour; there they spent the night 'in a respectable private house'. Before going to bed Mendelssohn wrote home, heading his letter 'On one of the Hebrides'. The letter contained a famous entence and twenty bars of music: 'In order to make you understand how extraordinarily the Hebrides have affected me, I have written down the following which came into my mind'

This was the first summer that steamer trips to Staffa and Iona had been advertised, and Mendelssohn had planned such a trip before leaving Edinburgh, but it cannot have been Staffa and Iona that so 'extraordinarily affected' him because he did not set eyes on them until the following day. Those evocative bars were inspired by islands and sea between Fort William and Oban or (more probably) between Oban and Tobermory.

However on 8 August the *Ben Lomond* sailed on into the open Atlantic, and the passengers were put ashore for an hour or so on both Staffa and Iona. Iona was inhabited and probably provided refreshment, but Staffa is uninhabited, tiny and very rocky. Its one attraction is Fingal's Cave with its remarkable basalt pillars like organ pipes. Fingal was the Celtic hero of the translations from Ossian that Macpherson had published around 1760 – translations that were still admired on the continent, though suspected in Britain of being largely Macpherson's invention. Whether they were or not, there is no evidence to link Fingal with this cave. Then, as now, landing on Staffa was dangerous except in calm weather, and because the passengers did land (Klingemann mentions a stout old lady determined to go ashore in spite of the scrambling) it must then have been fairly calm. Yet Klingemann wrote, with all the smugness of the man who has not himself been affected: 'The Atlantic stretched its tentacles around us with increasing roughness, knocking us all over the place ... The ladies went down like flies and so indeed did the gentlemen; I only wish my travelling companion had not been among them, but he's on better terms with the sea as a composer than as an individual or a stomach.' Instead of circumnavigating Mull as it would today, the steamer returned from Iona past Staffa to Tobermory. Mendelssohn may have been in good enough shape to appreciate Staffa in the afternoon, but he can then have seen it only from a distance.

The point is of some interest. He called the first draft of his overture *Die einsame Insel* ('The Lonely Island') and on publication the full score was headed *Fingals Höhle*, and for these reasons it has often been assumed that Staffa was the lonely island and the chief inspirer of the music. This is possible but unlikely. In Mendelssohn's published letters there is no mention of Staffa; all he seems to have remembered of 8 August was 'the most fearful sea-sickness'. Furthermore he is said to have disliked the catchpenny title his publishers foisted on him, and the probable reason is that Fingal's Cave did *not* inspire the music, Staff was *not* the lonely island; as has been shown above, the main theme had come to him elsewhere. Mull itself looks extremely lonely from the sea, as well as splendidly beautiful. If this seems too large an island, there are much smaller ones in the vicinity; for instance Calvé, just outside Tobermory harbour. The passengers had expected to be back in Oban late on the Satufday, but the steamer was far behind schedule and the captain anchored for the night in Tobermory Harbour. Very early on the Sunday morning the *Ben Lomond* sailed for Oban, and Mendelssohn and Klingemann immediately set off for Glasgow.

Mendelssohn did not compose his best works as fluently as has sometimes been supposed. He took nearly three years over his *Hebrides* overture, writing out two quite different versions of it; each of the MSS contains many alterations. He finished the first version in Rome on 16 December 1830, and it is headed *Die Hebriden*, but someone took a copy of this MS before Mendelssohn had made most of the alterations, and this copy is headed *Die einsame Insel.* More than a year later, on 21 January 1832, Mendelssohn wrote to his sister Fanny and told her that he still considered the overture unfinished. 'The loud D major section in the middle is very stupid, and the so-called development smacks more of counterpoint than of oil and seagulls and dead fish; and it should be just the opposite.' With a London concert in view he was already working on his second version of the overture, and this had its first performance on 14 May at a Philharmonic Concert with the composer conducting. In the light of this performance he made a few further adjustments, and the score was finally completed in London on 20 June 1832, as he noted on the MS. In the first edition of his Dictionary Sir George Grove mentioned that the published score and parts did not always agree, for instance in bars 7 and 87. No doubt this was because the published parts had been taken from those used at the first performance and took no account of the later adjustments.

Mendelssohn's surprising wish that his music should express the realities as well as the beauties of the Hebrides makes one wonder if he ever managed to make it do so to his own satisfaction. The calm sea of his second subject and the storm music are obvious to every listener, but where is the oil? Perhaps bars 149ff represent the chugging of the little paddle-steamer. There is evidence that Mendelssohn was very interested in the new steamers, and indeed in machinery of all kinds, but it must be added that this passage was already present in A.

The facts about the two versions of the overture can be summarized as follows:

A *Die Hebriden.* MS finished in Rome 16 December 1830; never printed, but this version was performed at the Crystal Palace, London, 14 October 1871. MS published photographically in Basle in 1948 (the British Museum copy is Hirsch M 281). While it was owned by Moscheles, Gounod added a minim D in bar 3, bottom stave, and wrote underneath that he thought it had been left out by mistake. Before many of the alterations were made, someone made a copy of this score; it is called *Die einsame Insel,* carries no date, and is now deposited in the Bodleian Library, Oxford.

B *Die Hebriden.* MS dated London 20 June 1832; a very free revision of A; substantially the version performed in London on 14 May 1832. It was published in full score in 1835 by Breitkopf & Härtel under the title *Fingals Höhle*; the parts had appeared the previous year under the much-to-be-preferred title *Die Hebriden.*

Information about Mendelssohn's travels is taken or deduced from the letters he and Klingemann wrote, and from Mendelssohn's diaries and dated pencil sketches, now in the Bodleian Library, Oxford. Information about steamer trips in 1829 is taken from *West Highland Steamers* by Duckworth and Langyard (3rd ed., Glasgow 1967), and verbally from Anthony Browning of Kelvingrove Museum, Glasgow.

Roger Fiske

Vorwort

Felix Weingartner stellte im Jahre 1909 sehr scharfsinnig fest: „Hätte Mendelssohn seinen einsätzigen Orchesterstücken den glücklichen Titel ‚Symphonische Dichtung' gegeben, den Liszt später erfunden hat, so würde er heute wahrscheinlich als Schöpfer der Programm-Musik gefeiert und hätte seinen Platz am Anfang der neuen statt am Ende der alten Periode unserer Kunst. Er hieße dann der ‚erste Moderne' anstatt der ‚letzte Klassiker'."

Die Opernouvertüre des 18. Jahrhunderts brachte zwei Nachfolger hervor. Die Sinfonie, deren Ursprünge nicht ganz so offensichtlich sind, entstand aus der dreisätzigen italienischen Opernouvertüre des Barock und entwickelte sich mit Haydn und Beethoven zu einer viersätzigen großen ernsthaften und abstrakten Musikform. Durch Beethoven wurde die Verbindung der Ouvertüre zum Theater und zur Oper noch einmal unterbrochen, wie man an etwa zehn Beispielen sehen kann. Er komponierte zwar Ballett- und Opernouvertüren, wie z. B. *Prometheus* oder *Egmont*, aber die Ouvertüre zu dem Schauspiel *Coriolan* (op. 62) wurde interessanterweise durch ein Konzert im Palast des Fürsten Lobkowitz im März 1807 bekannt. Da dieses Konzert vor der ersten Bühnenaufführung stattfand, war *Coriolan* genau genommen die erste Konzertouvertüre.

Beethovens Konzertouvertüren – einschließlich op. 115, ein Werk „zu jeder Gelegenheit oder zum Gebrauch im Konzert" – waren jedoch keine programmatischen Werke und haben daher nicht den Weg für die symphonische Dichtung bereitet, die später im 19. Jahrhundert entstanden ist. Weber hat die Ouvertüren erfolgloser Opern zu eigenständigen Ouvertüren umgearbeitet und bei Schubert sind Ouvertüren entstanden, indem er eine Reihe von Beispielen aus früheren orchestralen Ideen verwendet hat.

Die Werke, die Mendelssohn im Jahr 1835 gemeinsam unter dem Titel *Drei Konzertouvertüren* veröffentlicht hat, scheinen dagegen die Einführung einer neuen Gattung darzustellen. Sicherlich ist die Ouvertüre *Die Hebriden* vor allem ein Stimmungsbild, das als Antwort auf seine Reise zu den westlichen Inseln Schottlands zu verstehen ist; sie ist aber auch nicht ganz ohne Bezug zu *Meeresstille und glückliche Fahrt*, einem Werk, das im gleichen Band erschienen ist. *Ein Sommernachtstraum* bringt jedoch Anklänge an ein Bühnenwerk zum Ausdruck, obwohl der Komponist nicht beabsichtigt hatte, das Werk als Vorspiel zu Shakespeares Theaterstück zu verwenden. Als Sechzehnjähriger ging Mendelssohn im Jahre 1826 mehr noch als Beethoven einen neuen Weg und entwickelte eine neue musikalische Kompositionsform und Gattung.

Nach der Entstehung von Mendelssohns *Ein Sommernachtstraum* und vor der Veröffentlichung zusammen mit *Die Hebriden* und *Meeresstille und glückliche Fahrt* hatte Berlioz eine Reihe von Ouvertüren geschrieben, die zwar weniger programmatisch sind, aber dazu beigetragen haben, diese neue Gattung mit zu begründen: *Waverley, Intrata di Rob-Roy* und natürlich die „grande ouverture" zu Shakespeares *Le roi Lear*. Es gibt weitere Beispiele von Schumann, dem englischen Komponisten Sterndale Bennett und natürlich von Wagner, einschließlich seiner *Faust*-Ouvertüre aus dem Jahr 1840, die er später überarbeitet hat. Mendelssohn spielte eine Vorreiterrolle, indem er aus dem Schatten Beethovens herausgetreten ist und die programmatische Konzertouvertüre entwickelt hat. Damit bereitete er den Weg für die symphonische Dichtung, die Liszt dann in den 1840er und 1850er Jahren entwickelt hat.

Ouvertüre zu Shakespeares Sommernachtstraum, *op. 21*

komponiert: 1826 in Berlin
Uraufführung: Privataufführung im Hause Mendelssohn, Berlin, im November 1826; erste öffentliche Aufführung in Stettin (Szczecin) am 20. Februar 1827 unter der Leitung von Carl Loewe
Originalverlag: Breitkopf & Härtel, Leipzig; Stimmen 1832, Partitur 1835
Orchesterbesetzung: 2 Flöten, 2 Oboen, 2 Klarinetten, 2 Fagotte – 2 Hörner, 2 Trompeten, Ophicleide – Pauken – Streicher
Spieldauer: etwa 12 Minuten

„Musik her! Schlafbeschwörende Musik!", sagt Titania im 4. Aufzug von Shakespeares *Ein Sommernachtstraum*; und es ist das scheinbar ferne Rascheln der Flügel einer Elfe, welches nach vier magischen Bläserakkorden zu Beginn von Mendelssohns Ouvertüre das schläfrige Traumbild heraufbeschwört. Opernouvertüren hatten oft mit einer langsamen Einleitung begonnen. In diesem Fall wurde sie auf die kleinsten Gesten reduziert, wie man es auch bei Rossini und sogar in Beethovens *Coriolan* findet.

Obwohl die Musik die Ereignisse aus Shakespeares Theaterstück sehr genau widerspiegelt, engt sich der Komponist in seinen Ideen selbst ein, indem er die herkömmliche musikalische Struktur der Sonatenform verwendet. Im Anschluss an die Anfangsakkorde werden in der Exposition (T. 8–250) der Ouvertüre vier Themen vorgestellt. Die erste Themengruppe in der Tonika E-Dur beschreibt den spielerischen Tanz der Elfen und Feen im Wald bei Athen. Das große Fortissimo stellt die Szene im Palast von Theseus im ersten Aufzug des Theaterstücks dar (T. 62). Darauf folgt eine markante absteigende Tonleiter in halben Noten, die in verschiedenen Formen im ganzen Werk erscheint. Die geteilten Streicher im Pianissimo ergeben eine wunderbare feine Orchestrierung, ein Beweis für die frühen Fähigkeiten und die Fantasie des Komponisten. Der abrupte Wechsel zum vollständigen Orchester im Fortissimo ist ebenso wirkungsvoll. Die zweite Themengruppe in der Dominanttonart beinhaltet das chorartige Liebesthema, das Hermia und Lysander sowie Helena und Demetrius darstellt. Es mündet in eine Passage mit chromatisch absteigenden Terzen. Zu den hämmernden Oktaven auf dem Ton h (T. 197) spielen die Violinen und Flöten in Terzen im Fortissimo. Sie scheinen die Gruppe der Rüpel darzustellen, die später im 5. Aufzug ein „Theaterstück im Theaterstück", *Pyramus und Thisbe*, aufführen werden. Wir hören hier auch in Form von herabstürzenden Dezimen (T. 214) das Gebrüll von „Zettel“ mit seiner Eselskopf-Maske (3. Aufzug, 1. Szene). Die Exposition wird natürlich nicht wiederholt, denn in einem Werk, das eine Geschichte erzählt, würde dies wenig Sinn haben. Auch für die Sonatenform der Ouvertüre aus Beethovens Zeit war dies nicht charakteristisch.

Der zurückhaltende Durchführungsteil des Werkes im Piano/Pianissimo versetzt uns direkt in die Wälder von Athen, die die Kulisse für die zentralen Ereignisse in Shakespeares Theaterstück bilden. Die Wiederkehr des ersten Themas zeigt uns, dass wir uns ohne Zweifel in Oberons Elfen-Königreich befinden. Die absteigende Tonleiter, die auf das zweite Thema in der Exposition antwortet, lockt uns mit schleichenden Viertelnoten im Pizzicato – Violinen und Celli unisono in Oktaven – weiter in den Wald hinein. Die verzweifelte fragmentarische Anlehnung an den Schluss des Liebesthemas – wie die zerschmetterten Melodiefragmente in der Kavatine aus Beethovens Streichquartett op. 130 in B-Dur – erinnern uns am Ende der Durchführung an die unter einem schlechten Stern stehende Liebe. Schließlich erscheinen vor der Reprise erneut die Eröffnungsakkorde der Ouvertüre.

Die Reprise verweist nach dem Elfentanz im Pianissimo nicht auf den Glanz von Theseus Palast. Stattdessen verschmilzt die Wiederkehr des ersten Themas mit dem Ende der Überleitung der Exposition und führt uns wieder direkt in das Liebesthema, dieses Mal natürlich in der Tonika. Wie im 5. Aufzug, dem letzten in Shakespeares Theaterstück, treten „Squenz“, „Zettel“ und „Schnauz“ hervor und führen ihr Theaterstück auf. Um diese Szene darzustellen, erklingen bei Mendelssohn ein Oktav-Bordun auf dem Ton e im Fortissimo und eine rustikale Passage im Musette-Stil, die mit „Zettels“ brüllenden Nonen und Dezimen abschließt. Wie zuvor wird der Streicherabschnitt geschickt gestaltet, indem das Portamento für quasi-komische Effekte verwendet wird. Theseus erscheint schließlich in T. 586. Dazu erklingen eng geführte Fanfaren, die von den Bläsern und Streichern eingeworfen werden (T. 597–606). Die Coda der Ouvertüre entgleitet mit schnellen Achtelnoten in den Streichern leise in die im Licht der untergehenden Sonne leuchtende Welt der Elfen, während die Akkorde weiterhin breit ausgehalten werden. Das zweite große Thema ist sehr ruhig und erscheint am Ende als eine Art Referenz an Carl Maria von Webers Oper *Oberon*. Das Lied einer Sirene aus dem zweiten Akt von Webers Oper wird in T. 663 verwendet und spiegelt in T. 667–669 die in Webers Lied verwendeten Triolen im 6/8-Takt wieder. Es scheint, als ob Mendelssohn hier an folgende Passage gedacht hätte: „Weißt du noch wohl, wie ich einst saß auf einem Vorgebirge und 'ne Sirene, die ein Delphin trug, so süße Harmonien hauchen hörte, daß die empörte See gehorsam ward…“ (Oberon, *Ein Sommernachtstraum*, 2. Akt, 1. Szene). Die Eröffnungsakkorde kehren schließlich am Ende des Werkes ein drittes und letztes Mal ganz geheimnisvoll wieder, um „mit der Morgendämmerung zu verschwinden“, wie Mendelssohn es später seinem Verleger Breitkopf & Härtel beschreibt.

Die erste öffentliche Orchesteraufführung der Ouvertüre fand am 20. Februar 1827 in Stettin statt. Nicht lange nach der Fertigstellung der Komposition im Jahr 1826 wurde sie aber schon bei Mendelssohn zu Hause aufgeführt. Im Autograph vom 6. August desselben Jahres wurde vermerkt, dass die Partitur in der ersten Julihälfte vervollständigt worden ist. Das Werk existierte zuerst in einer Version für zwei Klaviere, und in dieser Form soll es der Komponist Ignaz Moscheles im November 1826 gehört haben. Mendelssohn schätze die Ouvertüre sehr und dirigierte sie regelmäßig bei Konzerten, auch in London. 16 Jahre später kehrte er noch einmal zu der Komposition zurück. Im Jahr 1842 fügte er im Auftrag des preußischen Königs Friedrich Wilhelm IV. zusätzliche Sätze als Schauspielmusik zu Shakespeares Stück hinzu – einschließlich eines Nocturnes, Scherzos und Hochzeitsmarsches. Als die Ouvertüre *Ein Sommernachtstraum* sieben Jahre zuvor zusammen mit der Ouvertüre *Die Hebriden* und *Meeresstille und glückliche Fahrt* veröffentlicht worden war, hatte der Komponist das Werk Friedrich Wilhelm, der damals noch Kronprinz war, gewidmet.

David Lewiston Sharpe
Übersetzung: Uta Heipp

Ouvertüre Die Hebriden, *op. 26*

komponiert: 1830–33
Uraufführung: 14. Mai 1832, Philharmonic Society, London, unter der Leitung des Komponisten
Originalverlag: Breitkopf & Härtel, Leipzig; Stimmen 1834, Partitur 1835
Orchesterbesetzung: 2 Flöten, 2 Oboen, 2 Klarinetten, 2 Fagotte – 2 Hörner, 2 Trompeten – Pauken – Streicher
Spieldauer: etwa 11 Minuten

Am Freitag den 7. August 1829 begab sich Mendelssohn mit seinem Freund Carl Klingemann in der Frühe auf einen der neuen Raddampfer, die zwischen Inverness und Glasgow durch den damals erst kürzlich eröffneten Caledoniankanal verkehrten. Die vierzig Meilen lange Reise ging Loch Linnhe hinunter bis nach Oban, durch eine der landschaftlich schönsten Gegenden Europas. Mendelssohn war damals zwanzig Jahre alt. Vom Hafen in Oban ging er eine Meile an der Küste entlang bis zu einer mittelalterlichen Riune, die Dunollie Castle heißt, und von der er begann, eine Bleistiftskizze zu machen. Es gelang ihm, Loch Linnhe und die fernen Berge von Mull im Hintergrund einzubeziehen. Doch hatte er nicht die Zeit, die Skizze zu vollenden, weil er und sein Freund noch einen anderen Dampfer erreichen mussten. Am selben Abend schifften sie sich auf dem *Ben Lomond* (70 Tonnen) ein, der sie von Oban bis nach Tobermory, dem einzigen Hafen auf der Insel Mull, trug. Dort verbrachten sie die Nacht ‚in einem respektablen Privathaus'. Bevor er sich zu Bett legte, schrieb Mendelssohn nach Hause und gab seinem Brief die Anschrift ‚Auf einer Hebride'. Dieser Brief enthielt einen berühmt gewordenen Satz und zwanzig Takte Musik: ‚Um Euch zu verdeutlichen, wie seltsam mir auf den Hebriden zumute geworden ist, fiel mir eben folgendes bei'.

Es war der erste Sommer, in dem Dampferausflüge nach Staffa und Iona angekündigt wurden, und Mendelssohn hatte einen solchen Ausflug schon geplant, bevor er Edinburgh verließ; doch können es nicht Staffa und Iona gewesen sein, bei denen es ihm so ‚seltsam zumute' geworden ist, denn er hat diese Inseln erst am folgenden Tag zu Gesicht bekommen. Jene stimmungsvollen Takte wurden durch die Inseln und die See zwischen Fort William und Oban oder (und das ist wahrscheinlicher) zwischen Oban und Tobermory inspiriert.

Jedoch am 8. August dampfte der *Ben Lomond* weiter und auf den offenen atlantischen Ozean hinaus und die Passagiere wurden für ungefähr eine Stunde auf Staffa sowohl wie auf Iona ausgesetzt. Iona war bewohnt und Erfrischungen waren daher vermutlich erhältlich, aber Staffa ist unbewohnt, sehr klein und sehr felsig. Die einzige Sehenswürdigkeit auf dieser Insel ist die Fingalshöhle mit ihren merkwürdigen Basaltpfeilern, die wie Orgelpfeifen aussehen. Fingal war der keltische Held der Ossian-Übersetzungen, die Macpherson um 1760 herausgegeben hatte. Diese Übersetzungen wurden immer noch auf dem europäischen Kontinent bewundert, während man Macpherson in Großbritannien verdächtigte, sie selbst erfunden zu haben. Wie dem auch sei, für die Verbindung von Fingal mit dieser Höhle gibt es überhaupt keine Unterlagen. Damals wie heute war es gefährlich, in Staffa anzulegen, außer bei ruhiger See, und da die Passagiere tatsächlich an Land gingen (Klingemann erwähnt eine beleibte alte Dame, die entschlossen war, sich trotz der Kletterei auf die Insel zu begeben), muss es wirklich ziemlich still gewesen sein. Allerdings schrieb Klingemann auch, mit all der Blasiertheit von einem, der nicht betroffen war: ‚ … die Atlantische (See) – das reckte seine tausend Fühlfäden immer ungeschlachter und quirlte immer mehr – … und überhaupt fielen die Ladies um wie die Fliegen, und eine und der andere Gentleman tat's ihnen nach; ich wollte mein Reisepechbruder wäre nicht unter ihnen gewesen, aber er verträgt sich mit dem Meere besser als Künstler, denn als Mensch oder als Magen.' Anstatt um die Insel Mull herumzufahren, wie das heute geschieht, fuhr der Dampfer von Iona, an Staffa vorbei, zurück nach Tobermory. Es ist möglich, dass sich Mendelssohn am Nachmittag gut genug gefühlt hat, um die Ansicht von Staffa würdigen zu können, doch kann er die Insel dann nur in der Ferne gesehen haben.

Das ist nicht ohne Bedeutung. Er gab dem ersten Entwurf seiner Ouvertüre den Titel *Die einsame Insel*, und als die Partitur veröffentlicht wurde, erschien sie unter dem Namen *Fingals Höhle*. Aus diesen Gründen hat man häufig angenommen, dass Staffa die einsame Insel war und dass sie in der Hauptsache die Musik inspiriert hat. Das wäre möglich, ist aber unwahrscheinlich. In Mendelssohns veröffentlichten Briefen wird Staffa nicht erwähnt. Von all dem, was sich am 8. August zugetragen hat, scheint er nur die ‚grässlichste Seekrankheit' in der Erinnerung behalten zu haben. Überdies heißt es, dass er den Reklame machenden Titel, den ihm seine Verleger angehängt hatten, missbilligt hat, und der wahrscheinliche Grund dafür ist, dass die Fingalshöhle die Musik *nicht* inspiriert hat. Wie weiter oben dargelegt wurde, war Staffa *nicht* die einsame Insel und das Hauptthema ist ihm woanders in den Sinn gekommen. Von der See gesehen, sieht Mull selbst höchst einsam und außerdem herrlich und schön aus. Sollte man diese Insel als zu groß ansehen, so könnte es sich auch um viel kleinere ganz in der Nähe handeln, wie zum Beispiel um die Insel Calvé, die gerade außerhalb des Hafens von Tobermory liegt. Die Passagiere hatten erwartet, spät am Samstag Abend wieder in Oban einzutreffen, aber der Dampfer hatte sich sehr verspätet und der Kapitän ließ das Schiff über Nacht im Hafen von Tobermory ankern. Am Sonntag früh dampfte der *Ben Lomond* ganz früh nach Oban und Mendelssohn und Klingemann machten sich sofort auf den Weg nach Glasgow.

Mendelssohn hat seine besten Werke nicht so im Fluss komponiert, wie man es mitunter angenommen hat. Die Komposition der *Hebriden-Ouvertüre*, die er in zwei ganz verschiedenen Fassungen niedergeschrieben hat, beschäftigte ihn nahezu drei Jahre lang und beide Manuskripte enthalten viele Änderungen. Er vollendete die erste Fassung am 16. Dezember 1830 in Rom und gab ihr den Titel *Die Hebriden*; aber irgend jemand verfertigte eine Abschrift dieses Manuskripts, ehe Mendelssohn den größten Teil der Änderungen vorgenommen hatte, und diese Abschrift steht unter dem Titel *Die einsame Insel*. Über ein Jahr später, am 21. Januar 1832, schrieb Mendelssohn an seine Schwester Fanny und teilte ihr mit, dass er die Ouvertüre immer noch als unvollendet betrachte. ‚Der Mittelsatz im *forte D dur* ist sehr dumm, und die ganze sogenannte Durchführung schmeckt mehr nach Contrapunkt, als nach Thran und Möven und Laberdan, und es sollte doch umgekehrt sein.' Für ein geplantes Konzert in London hatte er sich schon mit der zweiten Fassung der Ouvertüre an die Arbeit gemacht und diese Fassung wurde am 14. Mai erstmalig in einem der Philharmonischen Konzerte unter der Leitung des Komponisten aufgeführt. Diese Aufführung hatte zur Folge, dass er einige weitere Berichtigungen vornahm, und die Partitur wurde schließlich am 20. Juni 1832 in London vollendet, wie das Datum im Manuskript besagt. In der ersten Ausgabe seines Musiklexikons erwähnte Sir George Grove, dass die veröffentlichte Partitur und die Stimmen nicht immer übereinstimmten, wie zum Beispiel in den Takten 7 und 87. Das kam zweifellos daher, dass die gedruckten Stimmen auf den Stimmen beruhten, die bei der ersten Aufführung benutzt worden waren, weshalb die später hinzugefügten Berichtigungen im Druck nicht berücksichtigt worden sind.

Mendelssohns überraschender Wunsch, die Musik solle die Realität sowohl wie die Schönheit der Hebriden ausdrücken, lässt die Frage aufkommen, ob er je mit dem, was er in diesem Sinne erreicht hat, zufrieden gewesen ist. Die stille See seines zweiten Themas und die Sturmmusik sind für jeden Hörer deutlich genug, aber wo ist der Tran? Möglicherweise stellen die Takte 149ff. das Stampfen des kleinen Raddampfers dar. Es ist erwiesen, dass sich Mendelssohn lebhaft für die neuen Dampfer und überhaupt für Maschinen aller Art interessiert hat, doch muss hinzugefügt werden, dass diese Passage schon in *A* stand.

Die wesentlichen Angaben über die beiden Fassungen der Ouvertüre lassen sich folgendermaßen zusammenfassen:

A *Die Hebriden*. MS am 16. Dezember 1830 in Rom vollendet; nie gedruckt, aber diese Fassung wurde am 14. Oktober 1871 im Crystal Palace in London aufgeführt. MS fotografisch 1948 in Basel veröffentlicht (das Exemplar im British Museum trägt die Bezeichnung Hirsch M 281). Zu der Zeit, als es sich im Besitz von Moscheles befand, fügte Gounod ein D (halbe Note) im dritten Takt des untersten Liniensystems hinzu und schrieb darunter, er nehme an, dass diese Note versehentlich fortgelassen worden sei. Ehe noch viele der Berichtigungen eingetragen wurden, hat irgendjemand eine Abschrift dieser Partitur hergestellt. Sie trägt den Titel *Die einsame Insel*, aber kein Datum, und befindet sich zurzeit in der Bodleian Library in Oxford.

B *Die Hebriden*. MS gibt Ort und Datum, London 20. Juni 1832, an; eine sehr freie Bearbeitung von *A*; in großen Zügen die Fassung, die am 14. Mai 1832 in London aufgeführt wurde. Die Partitur erschien 1835 bei Breitkopf & Härtel mit dem Titel *Fingals Höhle*; die Stimmen waren schon im Jahr vorher unter dem Titel *Die Hebriden*, der dem anderen sehr vorzuziehen ist, erschienen.

Einzelheiten, die Mendelssohns Reisen betreffen, stammen aus den von ihm und Klingemann geschriebenen Briefen sowie aus Mendelssohns Tagebüchern und datierten Bleistiftskizzen (die sich in der Bodleian Library in Oxford befinden) oder sind aus ihnen hergeleitet worden. Die Auskunft über Dampferausflüge im Jahre 1829 stammen aus der Veröffentlichung *West Highland Steamers*, Verleger Duckworth and Langyard (3. Ausgabe, Glasgow, 1967) sowie aus mündlichen Angaben von Anthony Browning vom Kelvingrove Museum in Glasgow.

Roger Fiske
Übersetzung: Stefan de Haan

A Midsummer Night's Dream
Overture

Felix Mendelssohn Bartholdy
(1809–1847)
Op. 21

Allegro di molto

9
Vl.
I
II
sempre stacc.
sempre stacc.
div.
14
unis.
pizz.
Vla.
p
20
div.
pp
stacc.
stacc.
pizz.
pizz.
25
arco
30
unis.
35
Fl.
Cl. (A)
Fg.
Cor. (E)

41
Fl. 1 2
Cl. (A) 1 2
Fg. 1 2
Cor. (E) 1 2
I
Vl.
II
arco
pizz.
Vla.
pizz.
46
I
Vl.
II
arco
unis.
Vla.
51
Fl. 1 2
pp
Cl. (A) 1 2
[pp]
Fg. 1 2
[pp]
Cor. (E) 1 2
pp
I
Vl.
II
div.

57
A
Fl. 1 2
Ob. 1 2
Cl. (A) 1 2
Fg. 1 2
Cor. (E) 1 2
Tr. (E) 1 2
Oph.
Timp.
I
Vl.
II
Vla.
Vc. e Cb.
pp
ff
unis.
arco
63
2.
1.
tr

69
Fl. 1 2
Ob. 1 2
Cl. (A) 1 2
Fg. 1 2
Cor. (E) 1 2
Tr. (E) 1 2
Oph.
Timp.
Vl. I II
Vla.
Vc. e Cb.
ff
sf
tr

76
Fl. 1 2
Ob. 1 2
Cl. (A) 1 2
Fg. 1 2
Cor. (E) 1 2
Tr. (E) 1 2
Oph.
Timp.
I
Vl.
II
Vla.
Vc. e Cb.
a 2
ff
sf
tr

83
a 2
Fl. 1 2
ff
Ob. 1 2
Cl. (A) 1 2
Fg. 1 2
Cor. (E) 1 2
Tr. (E) 1 2
Oph.
Timp.
I
Vl.
II
Vla.
Vc. e Cb.

90
a 2
Fl. 1 2
sf
Ob. 1 2
sf
Cl. (A) 1 2
sf
a 2
Fg. 1 2
sf
Cor. (E) 1 2
Tr. (E) 1 2
Oph.
Timp.
I
Vl.
II
f
cresc.
Vla.
f
cresc.
Vc. e Cb.
[>]
f
cresc.

97
Fl. 1 2
Ob. 1 2
Cl. (A) 1 2
Fg. 1 2
Cor. (E) 1 2
Vl. I II
Vla.
Vc.
Cb.
1.
a 2
f
ff
103
Oph.

110
Fl. 1 2
Ob. 1 2
Cl. (A) 1 2
a 2
Fg. 1 2
Cor. (E) 1 2
Tr. (E) 1 2
Oph.
Timp.
I
Vl.
II
Vla.
Vc.
Vc. e Cb.
f
cresc.
ff
tr
f cresc.

117
B
Fl. 1 2
Ob. 1 2
Cl. (A) 1 2
Fg. 1 2
Cor. (E) 1 2
Tr. (E) 1 2
Oph.
Timp.
I
Vl.
II
Vla.
Vc.
e Cb.
p
sf
ff
1.
tr

124
Fl. 1 2
Cl. (A) 1 2
Fg. 1 2
Cor. (E) 1 2
1.
Oph.
I
Vl.
II
pp
Vla.
Vc. e Cb.
pizz.
p
129
Solo
arco
Vla.
Vc.

136
Fl. 1 2
Cl. (A) 1 2
Fg. 1 2
Cor. (E) 1 2
Vl. I II
Vla.
Vc.
Vc. e Cb.
pp
p
div.
144
153

161
Fl. 1 2
Ob. 1 2
Cl. (A) 1 2
a 2
Fg. 1 2
Cor. (E) 1 2
Tr. (E) 1 2
Oph.
Timp.
I
Vl.
II
Vla.
Vc.
e Cb.
cresc.

168
Fl. 1 2
Ob. 1 2
Cl. (A) 1 2
Fg. 1 2
Cor. (E) 1 2
Tr. (E) 1 2
Timp.
I
Vl.
II
Vla.
Vc.
Vc. e Cb.
f
mf
p
dolce
pizz.

176
Fl. 1 2
Ob. 1 2
Cl. (A) 1 2
Fg. 1 2
Cor. (E) 1 2
Tr. (E) 1 2
Timp.
I
Vl.
II
Vla.
Vc.
Vc. e Cb.
pp
cresc.
mf
p
arco
184
più f
f

191
Fl. 1 2
Ob. 1 2
Cl. (A) 1 2
Fg. 1 2
Cor. (E) 1 2
Tr. (E) 1 2
Oph.
Timp.
I
Vl.
II
Vla.
Vc. e Cb.
a 2
ff
f
C
198

205
Ob. 1 2
Cl. (A) 1 2
Fg. 1 2
Cor. (E) 1 2
Oph.
Timp.
I
Vl.
II
Vla.
Vc. e Cb.
212
Fl. 1 2
Ob. 1 2
Ob. 1 2
Cl. (A) 1 2
Fg. 1 2
Cor. (E) 1 2
Oph.
Timp.
I
Vl.
II
Vla.
Vc. e Cb.

219
Fl. 1 2
a 2
f
Ob. 1 2
Ob. 1 2
f
Cl. (A) 1 2
a 2
f
Fg. 1 2
Cor. (E) 1 2
f
sf
Tr. (E) 1 2
f
sf
Oph.
Timp.
I
Vl.
II
Vla.
Vc. e Cb.

227
a 2
Fl. 1 2
ff
Ob. 1 2
ff
Cl. (A) 1 2
a 2
ff
Fg. 1 2
ff
Cor. (E) 1 2
sf
ff
Tr. (E) 1 2
sf
ff
a 2
Oph.
ff
Timp.
ff
Vl.
I
ff
II
ff
Vla.
ff
Vc. e Cb.
ff

235
Fl. 1 2
Ob. 1 2
Cl. (A) 1 2
Fg. 1 2
Cor. (E) 1 2
a 2
Tr. (E) 1 2
Oph.
Timp.
Vl.
I
II
Vla.
Vc. e Cb.
sf
f
tr

242
Fl. 1 2
a 2
ff
Ob. 1 2
f
a 2
ff
Cl. (A) 1 2
f
a 2
ff
Fg. 1 2
f
a 2
ff
Cor. (E) 1 2
ff
Tr. (E) 1 2
ff
Oph.
f
ff
Timp.
ff
I
Vl.
II
ff
ff
Vla.
ff
Vc. e Cb.
sf
ff

D
250
a 2
Fl. 1 2
Ob. 1 2
Cl. (A) 1 2
Fg. 1 2
Cor. (E) 1 2
Tr. (E) 1 2
Oph.
Timp.
div.
pp
stacc.
Vl. I II
Vla.
Vc. e Cb.
1.
p
255
unis.

260
Fl. 1 2
pp
Ob. 1 2
1.
Cl. (A) 1 2
Fg. 1 2
pp
Cor. (E) 1 2
Timp.
I
Vl.
II
unis.
pp
Vla.
pp
Vc.
pp
266
Fl. 1 2
Cl. (A) 1 2
1.
pp
Fg. 1 2
[div.]
I
pp
Vl.
II
pp
Vc.

272
Fl. 1 2
1.
pp
Ob. 1 2
1.
pp
Cl. (A) 1 2
Fg. 1 2
1.
pp
Vl.
I
II
div.
1. Cb.
pp
Cb.
277
Fl. 1 2
pp
Ob. 1 2
1.
pp
Cl. (A) 1 2
pp
Fg. 1 2
pp
Cor. (E) 1 2
1.
[pp]
unis.
unis.
Vla.
pp
Cb.

283
Fl. 1 2
pp
Ob. 1 2
p
pp
Cl. (A) 1 2
pp
Fg. 1 2
pp
Cor. (E) 1 2
pp
pp
Tr. (E) 1 2
a 2
pp
Timp.
pp
I
Vl.
II
pp
pp
Vla.
pp
Vc.
pp
Tutti Cb.
Cb.
pp

289
Fl. 1 2
1.
pp
Ob. 1 2
2.
pp
Cl. (A) 1 2
Fg. 1 2
Cor. (E) 1 2
a 2
con tutta la forza
ff
Tr. (E) 1 2
a 2
1.
pp
Timp.
pp
I
Vl.
II
pp
pp
Vla.
div.
pp
Vc.
pp sempre
Cb.
pp

295
Fl. 1 2
1.
pp
Ob. 1 2
1.
pp
Cl. (A) 1 2
pp
Fg. 1 2
pp
Cor. (E) 1 2
a 2
dim. poco a poco
Timp.
tr
pp
Vl. I
pp
II
pp
Vla.
Vc.
301
1.
Fl. 1 2
pp
Cl. (A) 1 2
Fg. 1 2
Cor. (E) 1 2
ff
dim. poco a poco
Timp.
tr
pp
Vl. I
pp
II
Vla.
pp
Vc.
pp
Cb.
pp

307
Fl. 1 2
Cor. (E) 1 2
ff
dim.
pp
Timp.
tr
pp
I
Vl.
II
pp
unis.
Vla.
pp
Vc.
Cb.
314
E
Fl. 1 2
pp
Ob. 1 2
pp
Cl. (A) 1 2
1.
pp
pp
Fg. 1 2
pp
pp
Cor. (E) 1 2
a 2
p
Tr. (E) 1 2
1.
pp
Timp.
I
pp
Vl.
II
pp
pp
Vla.
pp
Vc.
pp
Cb.
pp

320
Fl. 1 2
p
Ob. 1 2
p
Cl. (A) 1 2
p
p
Fg. 1 2
p
a 2
Cor. (E) 1 2
p
1.
Tr. (E) 1 2
I
Vl.
II
Vla.
p
Vc.
p
Cb.
326
Fl. 1 2
Ob. 1 2
Cl. (A) 1 2
Fg. 1 2
Cor. (E) 1 2
a 2
Vla.
Vc.

333
Fl. 1 2
Ob. 1 2
Cl. (A) 1 2
Fg. 1 2
a 2
Cor. (E) 1 2
Timp.
pp
div.
pp
Vl. I
pizz.
Vl. II
pp
Vla.
pizz.
Vc.
340
a 2
pp
pp
pp
pp
1.
pp
arco
pizz.
pp
(pizz.)
pp
pizz.
Cb.
pp

347
a 2
Fl. 1 2
Ob. 1 2
pp
Cl. (A) 1 2
pp
Fg. 1 2
pp
Cor. (E) 1 2
1.
pp
Timp.
pp
I
Vl.
II
arco
Vla.
pizz.
Vc.
Cb.
(pizz.)
355
a 2
Fl. 1 2
1.
pp
Cl. (A) 1 2
1.
pp
Fg. 1 2
1.
pp
I
Vl.
II
unis.
pp
Vla.
arco
Vc.
div.
arco
unis.
Cb.
arco

364
1.
Fl. 1 2
Cl. (A) 1 2
Fg. 1 2
Cor. (E) 1 2
I
Vl.
II
Vla.
Vc.
Cb.
pp
373
dim.
p
espress.

382
ritard.
Vl.
I
II
Vla.
Vc.
Cb.
pp
392
Tempo I
Fl. 1 2
Ob. 1 2
Cl. (A) 1 2
Fg. 1 2
Cor. (E) 1 2
p
div.
402
1.
pizz.

408
Fl. 1 2
Cl. (A) 1 2
Fg. 1 2
1.
p
mf
Vl. I II
div.
unis.
413
Cor. (E) 1 2
2.
Oph.
418
Timp.
arco
pizz.
423

428
Ob. 1 2
Oph.
Vl. I
II
pp
p
434
Fl. 1 2
Ob. 1 2
Cl. (A) 1 2
Cor. (E) 1 2
Oph.
Timp.
Vl. I
II
Vc. e Cb.
pp
unis.
div.
arco
pizz.
[pp]
1.
tr
440
Fl. 1 2
Ob. 1 2
Cl. (A) 1 2
Cor. (E) 1 2
Vl. I
II
Vc. e Cb.
p

446
Fl.
Ob.
Cl. (A)
Fg.
Cor. (E)
Vl. I
Vla.
Vc.
Cb.
unis.
pp
arco
pp
arco
p
1.
452
Vl.
I
II
div.
arco
p

459
Fl. 1 2
p
Cl. (A) 1 2
p
I
Vl.
II
Vla.
Vc.
Cb.
468
Fl. 1 2
1.
p
Cl. (A) 1 2
1.
p
Cor. (E) 1 2
p
I
Vl.
II
p
p
unis.
Vla.
p
Vc. e Cb.
p

478
Fl. 1 2
Cl. (A) 1 2
Fg. 1 2
Cor. (E) 1 2
Vl. I II
Vla.
Vc. e Cb.
cresc.
sf
486
a 2
Ob. 1 2
Tr. (E) 1 2
Oph.
Timp.
Vc.
Cb.

495
Fl. 1 2
Ob. 1 2
Cl. (A) 1 2
mf
Fg. 1 2
mf
Cor. (E) 1 2
pp
cresc.
mf
Tr. (E) 1 2
Oph.
Timp.
I
Vl.
II
p
cresc.
mf
p
cresc.
mf
Vla.
cresc.
mf
Vc. e Cb.
p
cresc.
mf
503
Cl. (A) 1 2
cresc.
f
cresc.
Fg. 1 2
cresc.
f
cresc.
Cor. (E) 1 2
cresc.
f
cresc.
I
Vl.
II
cresc.
più f
cresc.
più f
Vla.
cresc.
più f
Vc. e Cb.
cresc.
più f

510
Fl. 1 2
Ob. 1 2
Cl. (A) 1 2
Fg. 1 2
Cor. (E) 1 2
Oph.
Timp.
Vl. I II
Vla.
Vc. e Cb.
cresc.
f
ff
a 2
G
518

526
a 2
Ob. 1 2
Cl. (A) 1 2
f
Timp.
I
Vl.
II
Vla.
Vc. e Cb.
f
534
Fl. 1 2
ff
a 2
Ob. 1 2
ff
a 2
a 2
Cl. (A) 1 2
ff
Fg. 1 2
ff
Cor. (E) 1 2
ff
Oph.
ff
Timp.
ff
I
ff
Vl.
II
ff
Vla.
ff
Vc. e Cb.
ff

542
Fl. 1 2
Ob. 1 2
Cl. (A) 1 2
Fg. 1 2
Cor. (E) 1 2
Tr. (E) 1 2
Oph.
Timp.
Vl. I
II
Vla.
Vc. e Cb.
a 2
f
sf
tr

549
Fl. 1 2
Ob. 1 2
Cl. (A) 1 2
Fg. 1 2
Cor. (E) 1 2
Tr. (E) 1 2
Oph.
Timp.
Vl. I II
Vla.
Vc. e Cb.
a 2
f
sf
tr

556
a 2
Fl. 1 2
Ob. 1 2
a 2
f sempre
Cl. (A) 1 2
f
sf
f sempre
Fg. 1 2
f sempre
Cor. (E) 1 2
a 2
a 2
f
f sempre
Oph.
f sempre
Timp.
tr
I
Vl.
II
f
Vla.
Vc.
e Cb.

562
Fl. 1 2
Ob. 1 2
Cl. (A) 1 2
Fg. 1 2
Cor. (E) 1 2
Tr. (E) 1 2
Oph.
Timp.
I
Vl.
II
Vla.
Vc. e Cb.
a 2
f
tr
f sempre

569
a 2
Fl. 1 2
Ob. 1 2
Cl. (A) 1 2
Fg. 1 2
Cor. (E) 1 2
Tr. (E) 1 2
Oph.
Timp.
Vl. I II
Vla.
Vc. e Cb.
f
sf

578
a 2
Fl. 1 2
ff
sf
Ob. 1 2
ff
a 2
Cl. (A) 1 2
Fg. 1 2
Cor. (E) 1 2
Tr. (E) 1 2
f
Oph.
Timp.
tr
I
Vl.
II
Vla.
Vc. e Cb.

586
a 2
Fl. 1 2
ff
f
a 2
Ob. 1 2
ff
f
Cl. (A) 1 2
ff
f
Fg. 1 2
ff
f
Cor. (E) 1 2
ff
f
Tr. (E) 1 2
ff
f
a 2
Oph.
ff
f
Timp.
tr
ff
I
Vl.
II
ff
f
ff
Vla.
ff
f
Vc. e Cb.
ff
f

594
Fl. 1 2
Ob. 1 2
Cl. (A) 1 2
Fg. 1 2
Cor. (E) 1 2
a 2
Tr. (E) 1 2
Oph.
Timp.
I
Vl.
II
Vla.
Vc. e Cb.

602
Fl. 1 2
Ob. 1 2
Cl. (A) 1 2
Fg. 1 2
Cor. (E) 1 2
Tr. (E) 1 2
a 2
Oph.
Timp.
Vl. I II
Vla.
Vc. e Cb.
ff

611
Fl. 1 2
a 2
ff
Ob. 1 2
Cl. (A) 1 2
Fg. 1 2
Cor. (E) 1 2
Tr. (E) 1 2
Oph.
Timp.
con tutta la forza
Vl. I
II
Vla.
Vc. e Cb.

H
620
Fl. 1 2
Ob. 1 2
Cl. (A) 1 2
Fg. 1 2
Cor. (E) 1 2
Tr. (E) 1 2
Oph.
Timp.
div.
I
Vl.
II
Vla.
Vc.
Vc. e Cb.
625
1. Solo
Ob. 1 2
Cl. (A) 1 2
div.

631
1. Solo
pp
Fl.
Cl. (A)
Vl.
636
Ob.
641
I
Fg.
Cor. (E)
650
K
poco riten.
dim.
dolce

660
Cl. (A) 1 2
Fg. 1 2
Cor. (E) 1 2
Vl. I II
Vc. e Cb.
pp
pizz.
668
pp dolce
Vla.
arco
676
ritard.
Fl. 1 2
Timp.
p
tr

The Hebrides
Overture

Felix Mendelssohn Bartholdy
(1809–1847)
Op. 26

EAS 122

6
Fl.
Ob.
Cl. (A)
Fg.
Cor. (D)
Timp.
Vl.
Vla.
Vc.
Cb.
p
pp
tr
perdendosi
10
Tr. (D)

14
Fl.
Ob.
Cl. (A)
Fg.
Cor. (D)
Timp.
Vl.
I
II
Vla.
Vc.
Cb.
tr
f
dim.
p
sf
pp

18
Fl. 1 2
f
sf
Ob. 1 2
f
sf
Cl. (A) 1 2
f
sf
Fg. 1 2
f
Cor. (D) 1 2
Timp.
tr
f
I
Vl.
II
f
f cresc.
ff
sf dim.
f
cresc.
ff
dim.
Vla.
f
cresc.
ff
dim.
Vc.
f
cresc.
ff
dim.
Cb.
f
cresc.
ff
dim.

21
Fl. 1 2
a 2
Ob. 1 2
Cl. (A) 1 2
Fg. 1 2
Cor. (D) 1 2
Tr. (D) 1 2
Timp.
Vl. I
Vl. II
Vla.
Vc.
Cb.

25
Fl. 1 2
Ob. 1 2
Cl. (A) 1 2
Fg. 1 2
Cor. (D) 1 2
Tr. (D) 1 2
Timp.
I
Vl.
II
Vla.
Vc.
Cb.

30
Fl. 1 2
Ob. 1 2
1.
Cl. (A) 1 2
Fg. 1 2
Cor. (D) 1 2
Tr. (D) 1 2
Timp.
I
Vl.
II
Vla.
Vc.
Cb.
sf
p

34
Fl. 1 2
a 2
mf
cresc.
[1.]
Ob. 1 2
a 2
mf
cresc.
Cl. (A) 1 2
p
Fg. 1 2
p
Cor. (D) 1 2
pp
Tr. (D) 1 2
pp
Timp.
tr
pp
I
Vl.
II
p
Vla.
p
Vc.
p
Cb.

38
Fl. 1 2
Ob. 1 2
Cl. (A) 1 2
Fg. 1 2
Cor. (D) 1 2
Tr. (D) 1 2
Timp.
Vl. I II
Vla.
Vc.
Cb.
ff
p
pp
1.

A
41
Fl.
Ob.
Cl. (A)
Fg.
Cor. (D)
Tr. (D)
Timp.
Vl.
Vla.
Vc.
Cb.
div.
[unis.]
1.

44
1.
Cl. (A) 1 2
Fg. 1 2
dim.
a 2
mf cantabile
Tr. (D) 1 2
p
I
Vl.
II
dim.
pp
sempre pp
Vla.
Vc.
Cb.
p
48
Fl. 1 2
pp
[a 2]
sf
p

51
Fl. 1 2
[a 2]
Cl. (A) 1 2
[a 2]
Fg. 1 2
cresc.
sf
pp
p
I
Vl.
I
sempre pp
Vla.
Vc.
Cb.
55
a 2
Cor. (D) 1 2
II
mf
sf
p

59
Cl. (A)
Fg.
I
Vl.
II
Vla.
Vc.
Cb.
pp
sf
p
cresc.
63
dolce

67
Fl. 1 2
Cl. (A) 1 2
Tr. (D) 1 2
Vl. I
Vl. II
Vla.
Vc.
Cb.
pp
p
dim.
cre
73
Ob. 1 2
Fg. 1 2
Cor. (D) 1 2
cresc.
sf
mf
cre
scen
do
non legato
f

B
77
Fl. 1 2
Ob. 1 2
Cl. (A) 1 2
Fg. 1 2
Cor. (D) 1 2
Tr. (D) 1 2
Timp.
Vl. I
Vl. II
Vla.
Vc. e Cb.
ff
a 2
80

83
Fl. 1 2
Ob. 1 2
Cl. (A) 1 2
Fg. 1 2
Cor. (D) 1 2
Tr. (D) 1 2
Timp.
Vl. I II
Vla.
Vc. e Cb.
sf
f
a 2
tr

86
a 2
Fl. 1 2
sf
ff
Ob. 1 2
Cl. (A) 1 2
Fg. 1 2
Cor. (D) 1 2
Tr. (D) 1 2
Timp.
I
Vl.
II
Vla.
Vc. e Cb.

90
C
Fl.
Ob.
Cl. (A)
Fg.
Cor. (D)
Tr. (D)
Timp.
tr
sf
ff
Vl.
I
II
Vla.
Vc.
e Cb.

94
Fl. 1 2
Ob. 1 2
Cl. (A) 1 2
Fg. 1 2
Cor. (D) 1 2
Tr. (D) 1 2
Vl. I II
Vla.
Vc.
Cb.
a 2
ff
sf
dim.
p
pp
101
marc.

107
Fl. 1 2
f
dim.
p
Ob. 1 2
f
dim.
p
Cl. (A) 1 2
Tr. (D) 1 2
marc.
mf
sf
I
Vl.
II
Vla.
Vc.
Cb.
112
Fl. 1 2
a 2
f con forza
Ob. 1 2
a 2
f con forza
Cl. (A) 1 2
a 2
f con forza
f
Fg. 1 2
a 2
f con forza
f
Tr. (D) 1 2
mf marc.
I
sempre pp
Vl.
II
sempre pp
Vla.
Vc. e Cb.
sempre pp

117
a 2
Fl. 1 2
f
dim.
Ob. 1 2
1.
Cl. (A) 1 2
Fg. 1 2
Cor. (D) 1 2
f con forza
sf
Tr. (D) 1 2
I
Vl.
II
pp
Vc. e Cb.
122
Vla.
p
Vc.
Cb.

128
Cl. (A)
Fg.
Vl.
I
II
Vla.
Vc.
Cb.
1.
pp
p
dim.
[unis.]
134
Fl.
Cor. (D)
Tr. (D)
a 2
mf
cresc.

138
Fl. 1 2
Cl. (A) 1 2
Fg. 1 2
Cor. (D) 1 2
Tr. (D) 1 2
Vl. I II
Vla.
Vc.
Cb.
1.
f
p
dim.
142
Timp.
Vc. e Cb.
cresc.
pp
tr

146
Fl. 1 2
cresc.
f
1.
dim.
pp stacc. e leggiero
Ob. 1 2
1.
p
Cl. (A) 1 2
f
p stacc. e leggiero
Fg. 1 2
f
pp stacc. e leggiero
Cor. (D) 1 2
f
Tr. (D) 1 2
f
Timp.
f
I
Vl.
II
sf
sf
f
dim.
pp
stacc.
Vla.
f
pp
stacc.
Vc.
f
p
pp
stacc.
Cb.
f
p
pp
stacc.

150
Fl. 1 2
Ob. 1 2
Cl. (A) 1 2
Fg. 1 2
Cor. (D) 1 2
Vl. I II
Vla.
Vc. e Cb.
sempre pp
a 2
p
154
Tr. (D) 1 2
Timp.
pizz.
poco
a
poco
cresc
cre
scen

158
Fl. 1 2
sempre
cre
scen
Ob. 1 2
cresc sempre
Cl. (A) 1 2
sempre
cre
scen
Fg. 1 2
sempre
cre
scen
Cor. (D) 1 2
sempre
cre
scen
a 2
Tr. (D) 1 2
sempre
cre
scen
Timp.
sempre
cre
scen
I
do
arco
sempre cre
scen
Vl.
II
do
sempre cre
scen
Vla.
do
sempre cre
scen
Vc. e Cb.
do
sempre cre
scen

D
162
a 2
Fl. 1 2
Ob. 1 2
Cl. (A) 1 2
Fg. 1 2
Cor. (D) 1 2
Tr. (D) 1 2
Timp.
I
Vl.
II
Vla.
Vc. e Cb.
- do
f
cresc.
non legato

166
Fl. 1 2
Ob. 1 2
Cl. (A) 1 2
Fg. 1 2
Cor. (D) 1 2
Tr. (D) 1 2
Vl. I II
Vla.
Vc. e Cb.
a 2
f
ff non forza
ff
più f
sf
ff non legato
170

173
Fl. 1 2
Ob. 1 2
Cl. (A) 1 2
Fg. 1 2
Cor. (D) 1 2
Tr. (D) 1 2
Timp.
Vl. I II
Vla.
Vc. e Cb.
a 2
ff
f
sf
tr

E
177
Fl.
Ob.
Cl. (A)
Fg.
Cor. (D)
Tr. (D)
Timp.
Vl.
I
II
Vla.
Vc.
Cb.
a 2
dim.
p tranquillo

182
Fl. 1 2
Ob. 1 2
Cl. (A) 1 2
Fg. 1 2
Cor. (D) 1 2
Tr. (D) 1 2
Timp.
Vl. I II
Vla.
Vc.
Cb.
dim.
pp
p

187
Cl. (A) 1 2
Fg. 1 2
sf
Cor. (D) 1 2
Tr. (D) 1 2
I
Vl.
II
p
sf
sf
Vla.
sf
Vc.
sf
Cb.
sf
191
Fg. 1 2
sf
cresc.
I
Vl.
II
sf
cre - - scen - - - do
f
sf
cre - - scen - - - do
f
Vla.
sf
cre - - scen - - - do
f
Vc.
cre - - scen - - - do
sf sf sf sf
f
Cb.
cre - - scen - - - do
sf sf sf sf
f

195
Ob. 1 2
1.
p
dim.
Cl. (A) 1 2
tranquillo assai
1.
pp
Vl. I II
dim.
p
dim.
pp
Vla.
dim.
p
dim.
pp
Vc.
dim.
p
dim.
pp
Cb.
dim.
p
dim.
203
Cl. (A) 1 2
p
Vl. I II
pp
Vla.
pp
Vc.
pp
Cb.
pp
210
Cl. (A) 1 2
p
dolce
un poco rit.
dim.
Cor. (D) 1 2
pp
Vl. I II
pp
pp
Vla.
div.
Vc.
Cb.
pp

216
Animato in tempo
Fl. 1 2
Ob. 1 2
Cl. (A) 1 2
Fg. 1 2
Vl. I II
Vla.
Vc.
Cb.
1.
p
stacc.
dim.
cresc.
sf
pizz.
arco
220
a 2
Cor. (D) 1 2
Tr. (D) 1 2

F
224
Fl. 1 2
Ob. 1 2
Cl. (A) 1 2
Fg. 1 2
a 2
Cor. (D) 1 2
Tr. (D) 1 2
Timp.
I
Vl.
II
Vla.
Vc.
Cb.
arco
ff non legato

227
Fl. 1 2
ff
Ob. 1 2
Cl. (A) 1 2
a 2
Fg. 1 2
Cor. (D) 1 2
Tr. (D) 1 2
Timp.
I
Vl.
II
Vla.
Vc.
Cb.

231
Fl. 1 2
Ob. 1 2
Cl. (A) 1 2
a 2
Fg. 1 2
Cor. (D) 1 2
Tr. (D) 1 2
Timp.
I
Vl.
II
Vla.
Vc.
Cb.
ff
f
tr

235
Fl. 1 2
Ob. 1 2
Cl. (A) 1 2
Fg. 1 2
Cor. (D) 1 2
Tr. (D) 1 2
Timp.
I
Vl.
II
Vla.
Vc.
Cb.
f
tr

239
Vl.
I
II
Vla.
Vc. e Cb.
con fuoco
con fuoco
242
Fl. 1 2
Ob. 1 2
Cl. (A) 1 2
Fg. 1 2
Cor. (D) 1 2
Tr. (D) 1 2
Timp.
a 2
a 2
f
ff

245
Fl. 1 2
Ob. 1 2
Cl. (A) 1 2
Fg. 1 2
Cor. (D) 1 2
Tr. (D) 1 2
Timp.
I
Vl.
II
Vla.
Vc. e Cb.
a 2

248
a 2
Fl. 1 2
f
sf
Ob. 1 2
Cl. (A) 1 2
Fg. 1 2
Cor. (D) 1 2
Tr. (D) 1 2
Timp.
I
Vl.
II
Vla.
Vc. e Cb.
251

254
Fl. 1 2
a 2
ff
sf
Ob. 1 2
Cl. (A) 1 2
Fg. 1 2
Cor. (D) 1 2
Tr. (D) 1 2
Timp.
tr
I
Vl.
II
Vla.
Vc. e Cb.

258
Fl. 1 2
ff
Ob. 1 2
a 2
ff
a 2
Cl. (A) 1 2
ff
Fg. 1 2
ff
Cor. (D) 1 2
Tr. (D) 1 2
pp
Timp.
Vl. I
ff
II
ff
Vla.
ff
Vc. e Cb.
ff

Printed in China